Jumpstarters for Math Word Problems

Short Daily Warm-ups for the Classroom

By
ANNE STEELE

COPYRIGHT © 2007 Mark Twain Media, Inc.

ISBN 978-1-58037-400-2

Printing No. CD-404059

Mark Twain Media, Inc., Publishers
Distributed by Carson-Dellosa Publishing Company, Inc.

Table of Contents

   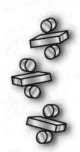

Introduction to the Teacher

Just as physical warm-ups help athletes prepare for more strenuous types of activity, mental warm-ups help students prepare for the day's lesson while reviewing what they have previously learned.

Many students often feel overwhelmed and nervous when they encounter word problems. The ability to solve word problems does not develop over a few weeks or months. It needs to be addressed virtually every day and in every grade. *Jumpstarters for Math Word Problems* is designed to provide daily opportunities to practice solving a variety of word problems typically found in middle school. Daily practice helps students improve their problem-solving abilities, which builds confidence and alleviates their anxieties in tackling word problems.

How the Book Is Organized

This book provides busy teachers and parents with a new set of problems for every day of the week. Each page contains five warm-ups focused on specific skills found in the typical sixth- through eighth-grade math curriculum. The warm-ups may be used for advanced or gifted students in grades four and five. Skills align with the National Council of Teachers of Mathematics (NCTM) Principles and Standards for School Mathematics. The problems on each page progress from basic to challenging and require students to use a variety of problem-solving strategies and mathematical reasoning, such as working backwards, guess and check, drawing a diagram, looking for patterns, identifying extraneous information, and logic. Some of the problems are multi-step. An answer key is included at the end of the book.

Tips for Using the Book

- **Class Warm-up:** Make overhead transparencies of individual activities and solve the problems orally with the entire class.

- **Individual Warm-up:** Reproduce one page for each student, cut out one activity and give to each student at the beginning of class. Have students solve the problem individually, and then share solutions as a class.

- **Individual Practice:** Give each student a copy of the entire page to complete day by day. Have students keep the pages in a three-ring binder or folder to use as a review resource.

- **Cooperative Group:** Reproduce individual activities and have students work in pairs or small groups to solve the problems. Working in groups gives students the support they need to interpret situations and represent them mathematically.

- **Learning Center:** Place copies of individual activities or the entire page of activities at a learning center for students to complete in their spare time.

- **Fill-ins:** Keep a file of copies or overhead transparencies of individual activities. Use as fill-ins when there are a few minutes remaining in the class.

- **Challenge, Extra-credit, Homework:** Reproduce individual activities or an entire page and give to students.

Introduction to the Teacher (cont.)

Tips for Improving Students' Problem-Solving Skills and Boosting Students' Confidence Levels

- Have individuals, pairs, or groups share with the class how they arrived at their answers. Sharing their strategies shows students that there is more than one way of solving problems and helps expand their critical-thinking skills.

- Have individuals, pairs, or groups write an explanation that describes the steps they took and invite a few to share their exceptional writings.

- Have tools, such as manipulatives, dictionaries, and calculators, available.

- Encourage students to follow problem-solving strategies:

  - Carefully read the problem, thinking about what it is asking.

  - Understand the problem. Identify relevant information and cross out irrelevant information.

  - Decide on a plan. Identify the operation(s) needed. Select a strategy, such as guess and check, solve a simpler problem, write an equation, work backwards, find a pattern, draw a diagram, make a table or organized list, use a model, or logical reasoning. Form an estimate of the solution.

  - Solve the problem and double-check your math.

  - Carefully examine your answer. Ask whether your answer makes sense. Look at your estimate to see if your answer is similar. Reread the entire problem.

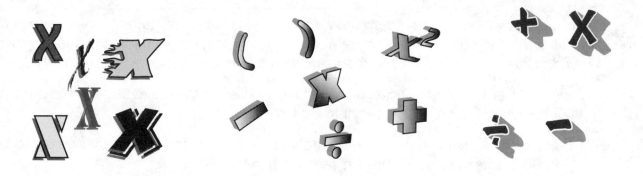

2

Math Word Problems Warm-ups: Add and Subtract Whole Numbers

Name/Date _____

Add and Subtract 1

Two thousand, seven hundred thirty-four dolls were sold in the first half of the year. Four thousand, one hundred seventy dolls were sold in the second half of the year. What was the total number of dolls sold in one year?

_____

Name/Date _____

Add and Subtract 2

Serina loves to read. She reads a chapter every night before going to bed. Last night she read chapter 6. If chapter 6 starts on page 73 and ends on page 94, how many pages did Serina read?

_____

Name/Date _____

Add and Subtract 3

A dealership had 216,417 vehicles in stock. The dealership had a June sale—a $2,000 rebate or 1.9% interest. The dealership received a shipment of 1,215 vehicles in mid-June. At the end of the June sale, there were 189,855 vehicles in stock. How many vehicles did the dealership sell in June? _____

Name/Date _____

Add and Subtract 4

Emily is training for the 100-mile MS Bike to Bay. During the first week of training, she cycled 75 miles. She cycled 84 miles the second week and 89 miles the third week. She cycled 98 miles the fourth week and 103 miles the fifth week. If Emily continues cycling in this manner, how many total miles will she have cycled at the end of the tenth week? _____

Name/Date _____

Add and Subtract 5

A. Karina ordered tulips, roses, and daisies from the florist. She ordered 36 more daisies than roses. She ordered 84 more daisies than tulips. She ordered 120 roses. How many flowers did she order altogether? _____

B. There are 189 students in the band. The difference between the number of boys and the number of girls is 27. How many boys and girls each are in the band?

_____ boys   _____ girls

3

Math Word Problems Warm-ups: Multiply and Divide Whole Numbers

Name/Date _____

Multiply and Divide Whole Numbers 1

A. Scott has been collecting comic books since the age of five. He collects about 30 books per year. If Scott is now twelve years old, about how many comic books does he have? _____

B. The comic book store ordered 1,295 comic books. If the books are packaged in boxes of 25, how many boxes will the publishing company need to mail the comic books? _____

Name/Date _____

Multiply and Divide Whole Numbers 2

A jeweler received an order for 9,000 rings. It takes about four hours to make 25 rings. If the jeweler works eight hours per day, how many days will it take her to complete the order? _____

Name/Date _____

Multiply and Divide Whole Numbers 3

A. Luc, Zac, and Emily are all reading books. Luc's book has 18 chapters, and each chapter is about 14 pages. There are 15 chapters in Zac's book, and each chapter is about 17 pages. Emily's book has 12 chapters, and each chapter is about 21 pages. Whose book is the longest? _____

B. Victor and his three friends were studying. Victor ordered three medium pizzas for a snack. There are eight slices per pizza. If each person eats an equal amount, how many slices did each person eat?

_____

Name/Date _____

Multiply and Divide Whole Numbers 4

Seth's father owns six restaurants. Each restaurant consumes 35 cases of fresh potatoes per week. How many cases of fresh potatoes will be consumed in one year? (Hint: There are 52 weeks in a year.) _____

Name/Date _____

Multiply and Divide Whole Numbers 5

Lou picked twice as many apples as Hugh. Kent gave half of the apples he picked to Tina. Tyra picked three times as many as Kent. Tina could not pick any apples; she has 50 apples. Hugh picked half as many apples as Tyra. Who has the most apples? _____

Math Word Problems Warm-ups: All Operations With Whole Numbers

Name/Date _____

All Operations With Whole Numbers 1

A. Five boys and two girls ate 24 sandwiches. Seven boys and four girls ate 36 sandwiches. Each girl ate the same amount of whole sandwiches. Each boy ate the same amount of whole sandwiches. How many sandwiches did each boy and each girl eat?

_____ boy   _____ girl

B. A baker makes nine dozen cookies. He divides them into 6-cookie and 2-cookie packages. If he wants to make the greatest number of each size package and the greatest number of total packages, how many packages of each size can he make?

_____ 6-cookie packages   _____ 2-cookie packages

Name/Date _____

All Operations With Whole Numbers 2

A farmer has 18 more horses than cows. There are 13 fewer cows than sheep. There are 15 cows. How many more horses does the farmer have than sheep? _____

Name/Date _____

All Operations With Whole Numbers 3

Twins, Henry and Helen, have a contest to see who can read the most pages in a week. Henry reads three pages on the first day and doubles the amount every day. Helen reads 30 pages each day.

A. Who reads the most pages? _____
B. How many more? _____

Name/Date _____

All Operations With Whole Numbers 4

Jun-Jee either ran 5 or 7 miles each day for 30 consecutive days. His total mileage during this period was 166.

A. How many days did he run 5 miles? _____
B. How many days did he run 7 miles? _____

Name/Date _____

All Operations With Whole Numbers 5

Elk Middle School has 264 students. There are 84 students in the eighth grade. There are 22 fewer seventh-grade students than sixth-grade students. Which grade has the most students? _____ How many? _____

Math Word Problems Warm-ups: Add and Subtract Decimals

Name/Date _____

Add and Subtract Decimals 1

In the final aerials contest, each contestant takes two jumps, with the highest combined score winning. Erin, Tamika, Kelly, and Maria all made it to the finals. Erin's scores were 94.99 and 96.4. Tamika made 100.81 and 96.58. Kelly scored 94.62 and 107.93. Maria scored 98.7 and 92.53.

Who won the contest? _____

By how much? _____

Name/Date _____

Add and Subtract Decimals 2

A snowboarding contest consists of three components: slopestyle, rails, and carving. Contestants take two runs for each component. The best score for each component is used to determine the combined score. If Tyler received scores of 29.2 and 29.6 in slopestyle; 26.3 and 25.9 in rails; and 27.9 and 27.0 in carving, what is Tyler's overall score?

_____

Name/Date _____

Add and Subtract Decimals 3

A diving tournament consists of five dives. Jiao is about to do her final dive and is the last to compete. She has scored 55.80, 56.40, 87.72, and 92.16. The current leader has a total of 371.52 points. What is the minimum number of points Jiao needs to win the tournament?

_____

Name/Date _____

Add and Subtract Decimals 4

Renton received 2.72 inches of rain less than Shelton but 2.2 inches more than Stampede Pass. Hoquiam received 3.99 inches more than Bellingham and 0.91 inches more than Renton. Shelton received the greatest amount of rain, 7.2 inches! How much rain did each city receive?

_____ Renton _____ Stampede Pass

_____ Bellingham _____ Hoquiam

Name/Date _____

Add and Subtract Decimals 5

A. Gerald's goal is to bike 60 miles per week. If Gerald biked 12.34 miles on Monday and 15.74 miles on Tuesday, how many more miles must he bike to reach his weekly goal? _____

B. Four boxes of pasta and one jar of tomato sauce cost $7.63. Three boxes of pasta and two jars of tomato sauce cost $8.81.

What is the cost of one box of pasta? _____

What is the cost of one jar of tomato sauce? _____

Math Word Problems Warm-ups: Multiply and Divide Decimals

Name/Date _____

Multiply and Divide Decimals 1

Brenda played basketball for 14 years. She averaged 30.1 points per game in her career. If she played 1,040 games, how many points did she score in her career? _____

Name/Date _____

Multiply and Divide Decimals 2

Gloria is planting flowers in a flowerbed with a length of 243.84 cm. The flowers must be planted 2.54 cm apart. If she wants to plant the flowers in a straight line the entire length of the bed, how many flowers will she need? _____

Name/Date _____

Multiply and Divide Decimals 3

On average, Sharon's running pace per mile is 0.75 times faster than Charlene's. If Charlene averages 9.32-minute miles, what is Sharon's pace per mile? _____

Name/Date _____

Multiply and Divide Decimals 4

According to Felicity's June electric bill, her daily average is 4.58 kilowatts per day. This is 1.8 times the amount used two years ago. Also, the price per kilowatt-hour has increased by $0.03. How many kilowatts per day did she use two years ago? _____

Name/Date _____

Multiply and Divide Decimals 5

Pedro is planning a trip to Lake Norman, a round-trip distance of 686.4 miles. His truck gets about 13.2 miles per gallon, and the gas tank holds 16 gallons. Gas costs $2.79 per gallon.

A. How many gallons of gas will Pedro need for his trip?

_____

B. How many tanks of gas will Pedro need for his trip?

_____

Math Word Problems Warm-ups: All Operations With Decimals

Name/Date _____

All Operations With Decimals 1

A. Subaru reported July sales totaling 17,959 units. This is an increase of about 0.02 compared to July of last year. About how many units did Subaru sell last July? _____

B. Seth is planning a 96.6 km bike ride. He usually drinks 0.18 liters of water at the end of every 4.83 km. At this rate, how many liters of water should Seth bring for the ride? _____

Name/Date _____

All Operations With Decimals 2

The Johnsons plan a seven-day driving trip from their house to New York City. Each day, they drive five hours and an equal distance. So far, they have driven 1,287.36 miles in four days. What is the distance from their house to New York City? _____

Name/Date _____

All Operations With Decimals 3

The library, shoe store, restaurant, video store, and movie theatre are all on the same street and in order from west to east. The distance from the shoe store to the video store is five times the distance from the video store to the movie theatre. The restaurant is halfway between the video store and the shoe store. The distance from the library to the shoe store is three times the distance from the shoe store to the restaurant. If the distance from the video store to the movie theatre is only 0.7 miles, what is the distance from the movie theatre to the library? _____

Name/Date _____

All Operations With Decimals 4

Mario wants to increase his daily mileage by four tenths of a kilometer. He currently is running 4.9 km four times a week. How many weeks will it take Mario to increase his weekly mileage to 34 km? _____

Name/Date _____

All Operations With Decimals 5

In the 4 x 400 m relay, each person on a four-person team runs 400 m. The times for Team North were: 49.19 seconds, 50.28 seconds, 49.81 seconds, and 49.73 seconds. Their combined time must be faster than 3 minutes 20.16 seconds to win the race. Did Team North win or lose the race? _____ By how much? _____

Math Word Problems Warm-ups: Add and Subtract Fractions

Name/Date _____

Add and Subtract Fractions 1

A. Julia has a bag of blue, red, and yellow candy. Two-fifths of the candy is blue and three-sevenths of the candy is yellow. What fraction of the candy is red? _____

B. Hector and David each bought a small pizza. Each pizza had six slices. Hector ate $\frac{2}{3}$ of his pizza. David ate $\frac{5}{6}$ of his pizza. What portion of the pizza did they eat altogether? _____

Name/Date _____

Add and Subtract Fractions 2

A. Greg's band made a CD of their hits. The first song is $1\frac{2}{7}$ minutes long. The second song is $3\frac{5}{7}$ minutes, and the last song is $2\frac{4}{7}$ minutes. How many minutes is the entire CD? _____

B. Greg's band spent $\frac{3}{4}$ of an hour setting up, $2\frac{5}{7}$ of an hour practicing, and $\frac{1}{8}$ of an hour tearing down. How long did the entire process take?

_____

Name/Date _____

Add and Subtract Fractions 3

The blue hiking path is a loop starting at the meadow with lookouts at Tumbleweed and Black Pine. The path is $16\frac{1}{8}$ miles long. It is $3\frac{1}{8}$ miles from Tumbleweed to Black Pine, and $6\frac{5}{8}$ miles from Black Pine to the meadow. How far is it from the meadow to Tumbleweed?

_____

Name/Date _____

Add and Subtract Fractions 4

A trail mix recipe of sunflower seeds, dried cranberries, mini pretzels, and multigrain cereal makes 3 cups. If Samantha puts $\frac{1}{4}$ cup sunflower seeds, $1\frac{1}{3}$ cups of mini pretzels, and $\frac{3}{4}$ cups of multigrain cereal in a bowl, how many cups of dried cranberries will she add to the bowl? _____

Name/Date _____

Add and Subtract Fractions 5

A. Raul ordered a pepperoni pizza, a mushroom pizza, and a cheese pizza for his math study group. Seven-eighths of the pepperoni pizza, one-half of the mushroom pizza, and $\frac{3}{4}$ of the cheese pizza were eaten. What portion of the total pizza was left? _____

B. The museum, bank, pet store, and post office are all on the same street. The post office is $5\frac{1}{2}$ miles west of the pet store and $2\frac{5}{8}$ miles east of the bank. The museum is $7\frac{2}{3}$ miles east of the bank. How far is it from the museum to the post office? _____   How far is it from the pet store to the bank? _____

Math Word Problems Warm-ups: Multiply and Divide Fractions

Name/Date _____

Multiply and Divide Fractions 1

A. Mr. Wilson has $\frac{4}{5}$ of an acre. He uses $\frac{1}{8}$ of the land for a garden. How many acres is he using for a garden? _____

B. Rita has 2 pies to serve to herself and her dinner guests. She serves each guest, including herself, $\frac{1}{6}$ of a whole pie. How many guests does she have? _____

Name/Date _____

Multiply and Divide Fractions 2

A. Marvin's cat eats $1\frac{7}{9}$ cups of cat food per day. If Marvin buys a bag that contains 16 cups, how many days can Marvin feed his cat? _____

B. A boarding kennel has 75 spaces. Of all the spaces, $\frac{7}{15}$ are for dogs, $\frac{1}{3}$ are for cats, and $\frac{1}{5}$ are for other animals. How many spaces are for each kind of animal? _____

Name/Date _____

Multiply and Divide Fractions 3

A. Trina made cupcakes. She took half the cupcakes to her book club meeting and left the remaining half at home. Trina's brother ate $\frac{1}{3}$ of the remaining cupcakes, and her mom ate $\frac{1}{5}$. How much of the total cupcakes did each eat? _____

B. On an average day, Trent's father spends $11\frac{1}{2}$ hours at work. Of this total, $2\frac{3}{4}$ hours are traveling to and from work. If Trent's father works Monday through Friday, how much time does he spend commuting to and from work in one week? _____

Name/Date _____

Multiply and Divide Fractions 4

Ada used fourteen beads to make an $8\frac{3}{4}$-inch-long beaded necklace. If the beads are the same size and cover the entire length of the necklace, what is the length of each bead? Reduce your answer to lowest terms. _____

Name/Date _____

Multiply and Divide Fractions 5

Naz made $11\frac{2}{8}$ cups of soup. She stored the soup in $1\frac{1}{4}$-cup containers. Then she delivered $\frac{2}{3}$ of the containers to her friends and put the remaining containers in the freezer. How many containers did she deliver to her friends? _____

Math Word Problems Warm-ups:
All Operations With Fractions

Name/Date _____

All Operations With Fractions 1

A. Joel had $\frac{3}{5}$ of a cake. Each piece he cut was $\frac{1}{20}$ of the whole. He served four pieces. How many pieces of cake are left? _____

B. Sasha is making new window treatments. She has three sliding glass doors that each require $6\frac{1}{8}$ yards of fabric. There are seven windows that each require $2\frac{1}{4}$ yards of fabric. Sasha buys 32 yards of fabric. Is this more or less than she needs? _____ by how much? _____

Name/Date _____

All Operations With Fractions 2

Charles is one-third as old as his father. In six years, Charles will be three-sevenths as old as his father. If Charles is less than 18 years old, how old is Charles' father? _____

Name/Date _____

All Operations With Fractions 3

The 2,842-seat performing arts center has three sections—orchestra, mezzanine, and balcony. The mezzanine has one-sixth fewer seats than the orchestra. How many seats are in the balcony if the orchestra has 1,218 seats?

_____

Name/Date _____

All Operations With Fractions 4

Brett made muffins for his grandmother, but he gave his friend Steve $\frac{1}{8}$ of the muffins. Then Brett saw Dori and gave her $\frac{1}{3}$ of what he had left. Then he saw Sheila and gave her $\frac{1}{7}$ of what he had left. By the time he arrived at his grandmother's house, there were only 12 muffins.
A. How many muffins did Brett make? _____
B. How many muffins did he give to each person?

_____

Name/Date _____

All Operations With Fractions 5

A carpenter drills five equally spaced holes in a $56\frac{3}{4}$-inch-long piece of wood. The two end holes are an equal distance from the center. If each hole is $7\frac{1}{2}$ inches apart, what is the distance from each end of the wood to the nearest end hole? _____

Math Word Problems Warm-ups: Money

Name/Date _____

Money 1

A. Colleen bought a package of hamburger for $5.83, a package of buns for $1.89, and a bag of French fries for $2.37. All together, how much money did Colleen spend? _____

B. Melissa bought a 22.17-pound turkey for $15.30. How much did she pay per pound? Round your answer to the nearest cent. _____

Name/Date _____

Money 2

A. Kirk buys two donuts for $1.39. He gives the cashier $2. The cashier gives him six coins back. What coins could these be?

_____

B. Noah buys a shirt for $22. He gives the cashier a fifty-dollar bill. The cashier gives him more than one five-dollar bill and twice as many ones as fives. What bills did he receive?

_____

Name/Date _____

Money 3

A. Charlotte, a waitress, earns $7.50 per hour plus tips. She earned $113.50, including tips, in 8 hours. How much money did she earn in tips?

_____

B. Martha's cellular phone service plan is $35.98 per month for 1,500 minutes and $0.12 for each additional minute. Martha's April bill was $58.42. How many additional minutes did Martha have in April? _____

Name/Date _____

Money 4

A. Broccoli costs $1.29 per pound, and lettuce costs $1.09 per head. Becky buys 3 pounds of broccoli and 2 heads of lettuce. How much change will she receive if she pays with a ten-dollar bill? _____

B. The mall parking garage fees are free for the first hour and $0.75 for each additional half-hour of parking. What will be the cost for parking if Eli parks his car for $3\frac{1}{2}$ hours? _____

Name/Date _____

Money 5

A. Carlsburg Middle School went whale watching. The cost was $8 per student and $10 per adult. The total cost for the whale-watching trip was $518 for 63 tickets. How many students went whale watching? _____ How many adults went whale watching? _____

B. Twins Mindy and Max want to buy their father a gift. If they combine their money, they have $105. Max is not happy about combining their money because he has $45 more than Mindy. How much money does each person have? _____ Mindy _____ Max

Math Word Problems Warm-ups: Customary Units of Measurement

Name/Date _____

Customary Units of Measurement 1

A. Jack and his father need 192 inches of rope to hang a tire swing from a branch of the old oak tree. The hardware store only sells rope by the foot. How many feet of rope do Jack and his father need?

_____

B. Alonzo has 3 cups of juice. Latrell has 2 pints of juice. Lydia has 4 ounces of juice. How much must Alonzo and Latrell give Lydia so they all have the same amount? _____

Name/Date _____

Customary Units of Measurement 2

A. Terrence and Anthony play on the Eagles' basketball team. Anthony is the shortest player at 5 feet 7 inches. Terrence is 6 feet 3 inches tall. How much taller is Terrence than Anthony?

_____

B. Shelly bought 7 pounds of sliced turkey. If she puts 2 ounces on each sandwich, how many sandwiches can she make? _____

Name/Date _____

Customary Units of Measurement 3

A. Bev takes 4 boxes of newspapers to the recycling center. The boxes weigh 90 ounces, 88 ounces, 93 ounces, and 97 ounces. The recycling center pays $0.20 per pound. How much money will Bev receive? _____

B. Earl had 3 quarts, 1 cup of crushed tomatoes. He used 1 quart, 2 cups to make spaghetti sauce. What amount of crushed tomatoes does he have left? _____

Name/Date _____

Customary Units of Measurement 4

A huge storm damaged about $\frac{1}{5}$ mile of fencing at Holden Ranch. Mr. Holden ordered a new fence that comes in 4-foot sections. How many sections of fence did Mr. Holden order?

_____

Name/Date _____

Customary Units of Measurement 5

A. Nate buys 5 pounds of apples. He uses 2 pounds, 6 ounces for apple strudel and 1 pound, 12 ounces for apple crisp. How much do the leftover apples weigh? _____

B. Dana made 12 gallons of her homemade chicken soup. She stores the soup in quart and pint containers. What's the greatest number of each size container that she can use?

_____

Math Word Problems Warm-ups: Metric Units of Measurement

Name/Date _____

_____

Metric Units of Measurement 1

A. Kelly drinks eight 250-milliliter glasses of water every day. How many liters does she drink in one week (7 days)?

_____

B. Leslie is making a beaded necklace 30 centimeters long. If she uses 10.5 millimeters-long beads, about how many beads will she need?

_____

C. Alicia made 7.5 liters of her homemade tomato soup. She stored the soup in containers that hold 375 milliliters each. How many containers did she use? _____

D. The distance from Larry's house to school is 2,700 meters. How many kilometers does he travel to and from school in a 5-day school week? _____

Name/Date _____

Metric Units of Measurement 2

Roger needs 3 kilograms of mixed nuts. The store only has 500-gram size packages. How many packages will Roger need to buy? _____

Name/Date _____

Metric Units of Measurement 3

Irene was making fruit punch. She poured in 20 containers of 475 milliliters of orange juice and 10 containers of 250 milliliters of pineapple juice. How many two-liter servings is this? _____

Name/Date _____

Metric Units of Measurement 4

Myra bought 3 liters of milk. She drank 450 milliliters in the morning, 250 milliliters in the afternoon, and 375 milliliters in the evening. How much milk does Myra have left at the end of the day? _____

Name/Date _____

Metric Units of Measurement 5

Catherine has 5.85 meters of fabric. She uses 91.5 centimeters to make a scarf and 152.5 centimeters to make a skirt. How many meters of fabric does Catherine have left? _____

Math Word Problems Warm-ups: Time

Name/Date _____

Time 1

Kimberly worked on her science project from 4:15 p.m.–5:30 p.m. Then she ate dinner and worked on the project from 6:30 p.m.–8:00 p.m. Then she watched television for an hour and a half. How much time did Kim spend working on her science project? _____

Name/Date _____

Time 2

A. Steph and Tracey are going on a bike ride that will take about 3 hours and 30 minutes. They want to finish their ride by noontime. What is the latest time they should begin their ride?

_____

B. Hiran's flight leaves at 2:05 p.m. and arrives at 5:20 p.m. Both times were in the same time zone. How long was Hiran's flight?

_____

Name/Date _____

Time 3

A. Last week, Matt worked at the bookstore for 2 hours and 45 minutes on Monday. On Wednesday, he worked 3 hours and 30 minutes, and on Friday 3 hours and 15 minutes. How many hours did he work last week? _____

B. Katy's class went on a trip to the planetarium. They left school at 9:00 a.m. and arrived at the planetarium 45 minutes later. They stayed for $2\frac{1}{2}$ hours. The bus trip back to school took one hour. What time did the class arrive at the planetarium? _____
What time did the class return to school? _____

Name/Date _____

Time 4

Samantha is making beef tenderloin for dinner. It takes her 5 minutes to season the beef. The recipe calls for roasting the meat for 10 minutes at 500° F; then reducing the temperature to 350° F and cooking the beef for 30 more minutes; and then removing the beef from the oven and letting it rest 10 minutes. It will take Samantha 7 minutes to slice the meat. To serve dinner at 7:15 p.m., what time should she start to prepare the beef tenderloin?

_____

Name/Date _____

Time 5

A. Peter drove to his grandparents' house for a visit. He left his house at 9:10 a.m. and arrived at his grandparents' house at 2:50 p.m. He stopped 45 minutes for lunch and 8 minutes for gas. How long did Peter actually drive to his grandparents' house? _____

B. The movie was 2 hours and 13 minutes long. If the movie ended at 6:10 p.m., what time did the movie start? _____

Math Word Problems Warm-ups: Using Measurement

Name/Date _____

Using Measurement 1

A. Tracy wants to hang lights around her outside balcony. She measures the lengths of the three sides: 9 feet 3 inches, $4\frac{1}{2}$ feet, and 6 feet 11 inches. What is the total length she needs?

_____

B. André bought 1 kilogram of cheese. Every day, he eats 56.6 grams. About how many days will it take André to eat all the cheese?

_____

Name/Date _____

Using Measurement 2

A. Three friends bought two gallons of milk. Each person drank 2 pints for lunch and 1 pint for dinner. How many quarts were left over?

_____

B. On a map, 1 centimeter represents 16 kilometers. The distance between Wapakanetika and Yarborough is 8.25 centimeters on the map. What is the actual distance in kilometers?

_____

Name/Date _____

Using Measurement 3

A. Ralph's plane was scheduled to take off at 12:06 p.m. However, the plane took off 35 minutes late. It took 5 hours 37 minutes to reach its destination. At what time did Ralph's plane reach its destination? _____

B. Rochelle made 5 liters of soup. Casey made twelve 375-milliliter containers of soup. Who made the most soup? How much more?

_____

Name/Date _____

Using Measurement 4

A. Arlene made fruit punch for the school picnic. She poured in 1 gallon of orange juice, 48 ounces of pineapple juice, 1 quart of apple juice, and 3 cups of cranberry juice. How many 1-cup servings of punch did Arlene make?

_____

B. Arlene makes a gallon of punch. She and her three friends each drink 1 pint of punch. How many cups of punch are left? _____

Name/Date _____

Using Measurement 5

A. The first half of Bryan's basketball game lasted 1 hour 10 minutes. The second half lasted 55 minutes. There was a 15-minute intermission between halves. If the game started at 6:30 p.m., what time did it end? _____

B. In one week, the veterinarian's office used 2 pounds, 10 ounces of dogfood out of a 12 pound, 4 ounce bag. How much dogfood was left in the bag?

_____

Math Word Problems Warm-ups: Angles

Name/Date _____

Angles 1

A. ∠LMN and ∠STR are supplementary angles. The measure of ∠LMN is 71°. What is the measure of ∠STR? _____

B. ∠P and ∠Q are complementary angles. The measure of ∠P is 50°. What is the measure of ∠Q? _____

Name/Date _____

Angles 2

A. ∠R and ∠S are supplementary angles. The measure of ∠R is 61°. What is the measure of ∠S? _____

B. ∠A and ∠C are complementary angles. The measure of ∠A is 68°. What is the measure of ∠C? _____

Name/Date _____

Angles 3

A. Chin was making a quilt. He cut a piece of fabric in the shape of an isosceles triangle. Before sewing the piece to the quilt, he measured the angles to make sure it was accurate. One angle measured 50°, and the other two angles were congruent. What is the measure of each of the congruent angles? _____

B. The Smiths' bedroom is in the shape of a quadrilateral. All four walls meet and form angles. Two angles measure 90° and a third angle measures 75°. What is the measure of the fourth angle? _____

Name/Date _____

Angles 4

Butch put a triangular-shaped flowerbed in the corner of his yard. The fence around his yard forms two sides of the triangle, and the angle measure is 90°. He put plastic edging along the third side. The measure of another interior angle is 53°. What is the measure of the third interior angle? _____

Name/Date _____

Angles 5

In quadrilateral DEFG, the degree of measure of ∠D is 40° more than the measure of ∠F and 25° more than the measure of ∠G. The degree of measure of ∠G is 90°. What is the measure of ∠E? _____

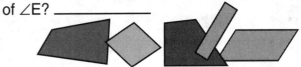

Math Word Problems Warm-ups: Perimeter and Area of Quadrilaterals

Name/Date _____

Perimeter and Area of Quadrilaterals 1

A. Joseph planted a rectangular garden in his backyard. The garden was 8.4 meters by 6 meters. How many meters of fencing does Joseph need to enclose his garden? _____

B. The Khuene family decided to put a fence around their rectangular backyard. The yard is 30 feet by 50 feet. The side with the house is one of the shorter sides and requires only 3 feet of fencing. How many feet of fencing will they need to enclose their backyard? _____

Name/Date _____

Perimeter and Area of Quadrilaterals 2

Natalie and Luis are painting pictures. Natalie's canvas is 18 inches on each side. Luis decides that he wants his canvas to have the same area as Natalie's but be rectangular with a width of 9 inches.

A. What is the area of Natalie's canvas? _____

B. What would the length of Luis's canvas need to be in order for the rectangular canvas to have the same area as Natalie's square canvas?

_____

Name/Date _____

Perimeter and Area of Quadrilaterals 3

Phan is painting his bedroom, which is 12 feet by 14 feet. The walls are 9 feet high. On one of the longer walls, there is a rectangular window that is 9 feet by 2 feet. One of the shorter walls has a door that is 6.5 feet by 3 feet. One can of paint covers about 400 square feet. If he puts one coat on each wall, how many cans of paint will Phan need to buy? _____

Name/Date _____

Perimeter and Area of Quadrilaterals 4

A. Juan is putting crown molding along the four walls of his dining room. The room is 18 feet long and 15 feet wide. One piece of crown molding is 94.5 inches long. How many pieces of crown molding will Juan need to buy? _____

B. Tad's bedroom is a square with a perimeter of 72 feet. What is the area of Tad's bedroom?

_____

Name/Date _____

Perimeter and Area of Quadrilaterals 5

It took Vincent 104 yards of fencing to enclose a square area around the swimming pool. The length and width of the fencing around the swimming pool are ½ those of the fencing enclosing his square garden. How many yards of fencing are used to enclose his square garden?

_____

Math Word Problems Warm-ups: Circumference and Area of Circles

Name/Date _____

Circumference and Area of Circles 1

A. Trevor needs a new bicycle tire. His tire has a circumference of about 113.04 inches. What is the diameter of his tire?

_____

B. Gene's frying pan is 13.5 inches in diameter. What is the circumference of his frying pan? _____

Name/Date _____

Circumference and Area of Circles 2

A farmer has three silos. The largest silo has a diameter of 24 feet. The radius of the smallest silo is one-third as big as the diameter of the largest. The middle-sized silo has a radius that is 2 feet greater than the radius of the smallest silo. What is the circumference of each silo? _____ _____ _____

Name/Date _____

Circumference and Area of Circles 3

A. Brad is putting an 8-foot diameter circular flower garden in his yard. He will put plastic edging along the flowerbed. How many feet of edging will Brad need to enclose his flower garden?

_____

B. How many square feet of land are in Brad's garden?

_____

Name/Date _____

Circumference and Area of Circles 4

A. Kelsey bought a circular rug that is 8 feet in diameter. The rug has a blue border and a red circular center that is 6 feet in diameter. What is the area of the blue border? _____
B. Macy measures a truck's tire mark for one complete revolution as 100.48 inches long. What is the diameter of the tire?

_____

Name/Date _____

Circumference and Area of Circles 5

A. Anna is covering the circular pool with a heavy-duty cover for the winter. The pool has a diameter of 24 feet. The cover extends 12 inches beyond the edge of the pool, and a rope runs along the edge of the cover to secure the cover in place. What is the area of the cover? _____
What is the length of the rope? _____

B. How many square inches greater is the area of a 30-inch circular mirror than an 18-inch circular mirror?

_____

Math Word Problems Warm-ups: Volume

Name/Date _____

Volume 1

Kim built a birdhouse shaped like a rectangular prism. The birdhouse was 10 centimeters wide, 12 centimeters long, and 21 centimeters high. What is the volume of the birdhouse?

_____

Name/Date _____

Volume 2

A pepper shaker is shaped like a cylinder. It is 13 centimeters high with a diameter of 3 centimeters. What is the volume of the pepper shaker?

_____

Name/Date _____

Volume 3

A. Reneé has a precious stone collection. She stores each stone in a 1.2-inch square velvet box. She then puts these small square boxes in one large wooden box that is 9.6 inches long, 7.2 inches wide, 3.6 inches high. This large box is completely filled with the small square boxes. How many precious stones does Reneé have? _____

B. Roberto made a sandbox. The sandbox holds 22 cubic feet of sand. The width of the sandbox is 5.5 feet. The height is 0.5 feet. What is the length of the sandbox? _____

Name/Date _____

Volume 4

Dorothy is making her famous strawberry preserves. She stores the preserves in cylindrical jars. One jar is 4 inches tall with a 2-inch diameter base. The other jar is 6 inches tall with a 3-inch diameter base. What is the difference in volume between the two jars?

_____

Name/Date _____

Volume 5

Sara shipped some books to a friend. The box was 10 inches wide, 15 inches long, and 8 inches high. What was the volume of the box?

_____

20

Math Word Problems Warm-ups: Surface Area

Name/Date _____

Surface Area 1

Len built a toy chest shaped like a rectangular prism. The width of the chest is 3 feet. The height is 2 feet, and the length is 5 feet. Len painted the outside of the chest blue. What is the total surface area he painted?

_____

Name/Date _____

Surface Area 2

The Albrights built an in-ground swimming pool shaped like a rectangular prism. The pool is 3 yards wide, 12 yards long, and 1.4 yards deep. The sides and bottom are covered with cement. What is the total surface area of the interior sides and bottom of the swimming pool? _____

Name/Date _____

Surface Area 3

Rex is wrapping a gift that is shaped like a cylinder. He uses solid blue wrap for the top and bottom and polka-dotted wrap around the gift. He uses the least amount of wrapping paper possible. If the gift is 30 centimeters high with a diameter of 20 centimeters, how much wrapping paper did he use to cover the gift?

_____

Name/Date _____

Surface Area 4

A. The surface area of a rectangular prism is 812 square centimeters. The width is 11 centimeters. The length is 20 centimeters. What is the height of the rectangular prism? _____

B. The surface area of a rectangular-prism-shaped toolbox is 5,050 square centimeters. It is 50 centimeters long and 17 centimeters high. What is the width of the toolbox? _____

Name/Date _____

Surface Area 5

A. Pam covers a cylinder-shaped lampshade with fabric. She does not cover the top and bottom. The lampshade is 15 inches high and has a diameter of 20 inches. What is the area she covers with fabric? _____

B. The surface area of a candle is 125.6 square inches. If the candle has a diameter of 4 inches, what is the height of the candle?

_____

Math Word Problems Warm-ups: Ratios

Name/Date _____

Ratios 1

A. There are 33 students in the Drama Club and 18 students in the Speech and Debate Club. What is the ratio of Drama Club members to Speech and Debate Club members? _____

B. There are 15 geese and 7 ducks in the pond. What is the ratio of ducks to geese? _____

Name/Date _____

Ratios 2

A. Lou loves to read. Over the summer, he read 9 fiction books and 20 nonfiction books. What is his ratio of fiction books to nonfiction books? _____

B. Emily has 17 shirts, 12 skirts, 5 pairs of pants, and 3 pairs of shoes. What is the ratio of pants to skirts? _____ What is the ratio of pairs of shoes to shirts? _____

Name/Date _____

Ratios 3

On Monday, the students in Mr. Wallace's class bought 12 hot lunches and 9 sack lunches.

A. What is the ratio of sack lunches to hot lunches? _____

B. The school cafeteria sold a total of 360 lunches on Monday. Based on the ratio above, how many lunches were hot? _____ sack? _____

The Happy Pet animal shelter houses stray cats and dogs. There are 55 animals at the shelter. The ratio of the number of cats to the number of dogs is 4 to 7.

C. Based on this ratio, how many animals are dogs? _____

D. How many animals are cats? _____

Name/Date _____

Ratios 4

Pearson Farm has 18 acres of apple trees, 12 acres of orange trees, and 5 acres of olive trees.

A. What is the ratio of orange trees to apple trees to olive trees? _____

B. What is the ratio of olive trees to total acreage? _____

Name/Date _____

Ratios 5

Brad and Alice were both running for student government president. One hundred twenty-eight students voted. The ratio of the number of votes for Alice to the number of votes for Brad was 5 to 3. Based on this ratio, how many students voted for Brad? _____ for Alice? _____

Math Word Problems Warm-ups: Proportions

Name/Date _____

Proportions 1

A. Perth Middle School is going on a field trip. School policy requires one _____
   adult chaperon for every 6 students. There are 360 students. How many
   chaperons will be needed?

B. The ratio of boys to girls in the marching band is 15:7. If there are 63 _____
   girls, how many boys are there?

Name/Date _____

Proportions 2

Teresa works for a newspaper. She has a photograph that is 9″ high by 12″ _____
wide. The photo is too large for the allotted space. She needs to reduce the
picture so the height is $4\frac{1}{2}$″. How wide will the picture be?

Name/Date _____

Proportions 3

A. A roadmap's scale shows 2″ is equals to 35 miles. Branton and Smallwood _____
   are 8″ apart. How many miles is it from Branton to Smallwood?

B. Bernice, a caterer, is preparing green beans for 2,330 people. Three _____
   pounds serves 12 people. If Bernice prepares 585 pounds of green
   beans, how many servings will she have left over?

Name/Date _____

Proportions 4

Mitchell was making fruit punch. The recipe calls for 3 parts orange juice to _____
2 parts cranberry juice and 1 part grapefruit juice. Mitchell pours 48 ounces
of cranberry juice into a container. How much orange juice and grapefruit _____
juice should he mix with the cranberry juice?

Name/Date _____

Proportions 5

A. A car manufacturer made 278,000 new cars. Two out of five of those cars are _____
   hybrids. Based on this ratio, how many of the cars were not hybrids?

B. It takes 4 people 18 days to build 12 computers. If two more people helped, _____
   how many days would it probably have taken to build all 12 computers?

Math Word Problems Warm-ups: Unit Prices

Name/Date _____

Unit Prices 1

A. Morgan bought a box of 50 chocolates for $16.50. What was the cost per chocolate? _____

B. Go Sports is offering a one-year subscription to their magazine at a low introductory rate of $14.99 for 12 exciting issues. What is the cost per issue? Round your answer to the nearest cent. _____

C. If this is $1.50 less than the newsstand price per issue, what is the newsstand price for one issue? _____

Name/Date _____

Unit Prices 2

A. Grace bought 2.38 pounds of rib-eye steaks at $5.99 per pound. How much did she pay for the steaks? Round your answer to the nearest cent. _____

B. Hector bought some grapes for $5.93. If the grapes were on sale for $2.49 per pound, how many pounds did Hector buy? Round your answer to the nearest hundredth. _____

Name/Date _____

Unit Prices 3

A. Anthony bought 8 cans of beans for $7.76. At this price, how much would 15 cans cost? _____

B. At the hardware store, one lightbulb costs $5.85, a 2-pack of lightbulbs costs $11.93, and a 6-pack costs $25.97. Which has the lowest unit price? _____

Name/Date _____

Unit Prices 4

A. At the grocery store, Alec had to choose between a package of twelve 14-ounce cans of broth for $5.04 and three 64-ounce cans for $3.84. Which package costs less per unit? _____

B. Andy paid $66 for 6 tulips and 18 roses. The next week, he bought 4 tulips and 7 roses for $29. What is the unit price for each kind of flower? _____

Name/Date _____

Unit Prices 5

A. The grocery store had two 2.5 gallons of water for $5.00, and a 24-pack of 16-ounce bottles for $3.99. Which is the better buy? _____

B. The Friendly Cleaners charged Laura $14.75 to have 3 dresses and 2 blouses dry-cleaned. The following week, she paid $15.50 to have 4 dresses and 1 blouse dry-cleaned. What is the unit price per blouse? _____ per dress? _____

Math Word Problems Warm-ups: Fractions, Decimals, & Percents

Name/Date _____

Fractions, Decimals, & Percents 1

A. Four-fifths of the students surveyed said they liked pizza for lunch. Seventy-five percent liked hamburgers. Which food did most students like? _____

B. At MusicLand, 18% of the music sold is classical, $\frac{1}{5}$ is rock, and 0.62 is country. What type of music sold the most? _____ the least? _____

Name/Date _____

Fractions, Decimals, & Percents 2

Students sold tickets for the school raffle. Aaron sold $\frac{1}{3}$ of the tickets. Valerie sold 30% of the tickets, and Nan sold 0.31 of the tickets. Each student had the same number of tickets to sell. Who sold the greatest number of tickets? _____

Name/Date _____

Fractions, Decimals, & Percents 3

Ella bought tickets at the carnival. She used 70% of the tickets for rides, 12% for food and drinks, and 15% to play games. She gave 3% of the tickets to her brother.

A. What is the ratio of rides to total tickets? Write your answer as a fraction and a decimal. _____

B. Which two activities make up $\frac{27}{100}$ of the tickets? _____

Name/Date _____

Fractions, Decimals, & Percents 4

Three candidates were running for class treasurer: Dwane, Mary, and Joyce. Dwane received $\frac{1}{4}$ of the votes. Mary received 1.8 times as many votes as Dwane. Joyce received 30% of the votes. Five hundred twenty students voted.

A. How many votes did Dwane receive? _____

B. How many votes did Mary receive? _____

C. How many votes did Joyce receive? _____

Name/Date _____

Fractions, Decimals, & Percents 5

Tara, Regina, Shane, and Tony had a carwash to earn money for charity. Tara washed 1.4 times as many cars as Regina. Shane washed 70% of the cars. Regina washed $\frac{4}{8}$ of the cars. Tony washed $\frac{1}{5}$ of the cars. They washed a total of 25 cars.

A. Who washed the same amount of cars? _____

B. Who washed the least amount of cars? _____

C. How many cars did Tony not wash? _____

Math Word Problems Warm-ups: Find Percents of Numbers

Name/Date _____

Find Percents of Numbers 1

A. Meena works at a car dealership where she makes 5% commission from her sales and earns $9.50 per hour. She sold a car for $22,500. What is Meena's commission from this sale? _____

B. Darren bikes 23 miles per week. To train for a bike marathon, he increases his weekly mileage by 12% from the prior week. How many weeks will it take Darren to reach his goal of 36 miles? _____

C. Esther tiled her bathroom floor with 60% black tiles and the rest white tiles. If the bathroom is 6′ x 4′, what area of the bathroom is white tile? _____

Name/Date _____

Find Percents of Numbers 2

A. Rox Theatre has 545 seats. If 20% of the seats are sold for the performance, how many seats are not yet sold? _____

B. The park's pond had 200 birds. Forty-nine percent were ducks, 26.5% geese, and the rest swans. How many swans were there? _____ ducks? _____ geese? _____

Name/Date _____

Find Percents of Numbers 3

In a survey of 300 students, 35% prefer to watch hockey, 48% prefer basketball, 12% prefer baseball, and the rest prefer other sports.

A. How many students prefer to watch other sports? _____

B. How many more students prefer basketball than baseball? _____

C. How many prefer hockey? _____

Name/Date _____

Find Percents of Numbers 4

Yesterday's News consignment store will try to sell your items for you. The store keeps 45% of the selling price, and you keep the rest. Peggy has Yesterday's News try to sell a rocking chair for her. The store sells the chair for $535. How much money did Peggy receive from the sale?

_____

Name/Date _____

Find Percents of Numbers 5

A. Oliver had a 3″ x 5″ picture that he enlarged by 195%. What are the dimensions of the enlarged picture? _____

B. Last year, Becker's Bakery sold 1,220 cakes. This year, the bakery sold 145% more cakes. How many cakes did the bakery sell this year? _____

Math Word Problems Warm-ups: Find a Percent

Name/Date _____

Find a Percent 1

A. Benjamin correctly answered 27 out of 35 questions on the math test. What percent of the questions did Benjamin get correct? Round your answer to the nearest percent.

_____

B. Ralph, a volleyball player, got 20 aces out of 50 serves. What percent of the hits were aces? _____

Name/Date _____

Find a Percent 2

A. Shelia went snowboarding. She spent $118 for the pass and snowboard rental. The snowboard rental cost $25. What percent of the total cost was the pass? Round your answer to the nearest percent. _____

B. Chloe spent $9 on a dress, $13 on pants, and $7 on a shirt. What percent of the total money spent was on the pants? Round your answer to the nearest percent, if necessary. _____

Name/Date _____

Find a Percent 3

Craig and Les love to play pinball. Craig scored at least 500,000 points in 6 out of the 8 games in which he played. Les scored at least 490,000 points in 7 out of the 8 games in which he played.

A. In what percent of the games in which Craig played did he get at least 500,000 points? Round your answer to the nearest percent. _____

B. In what percent of the games in which Les played did he score at least 490,000 points? Round your answer to the nearest percent. _____

Name/Date _____

Find a Percent 4

The recreation center offers 6 yoga classes. The classes are limited to 30 students each. During the first week of registration, 126 people registered for classes.

A. What percent of the total possible registration remains open? Round your answer to the nearest percent. _____

B. Of the 126 people registered, 63 have taken the class before. What percent of the registered students have taken the class before? _____

Name/Date _____

Find a Percent 5

Ticket sales for the Distinguished Speakers Series were 625 tickets to the season ticket holders and 130 tickets to new participants.

A. What percent of the total tickets sold were to season ticket holders? Round your answer to the nearest percent. _____

B. What percent went to new participants?

_____

Math Word Problems Warm-ups:
Find a Number When a Percent of It Is Known

Name/Date _____

Find a Number When a Percent of It Is Known 1

Marvin is earning money for summer camp. So far, he has earned $1,225 for doing yard work, which is 35% of the cost for summer camp.

A. What is the total cost for summer camp?

_____

B. How much more money does he need to earn? _____

Name/Date _____

Find a Number When a Percent of It Is Known 2

A. Fifty-eight people work the presses at Quick Printing Company. This is 40% of all employees. How many employees does Quick Printing Company have? _____

B. Twenty-five percent of Quick Prints' customers get flyers printed. If there are 32 flyer customers, how many customers does Quick Print have? _____

Name/Date _____

Find a Number When a Percent of It Is Known 3

A. Henry's baseball team won 36 games. If this is 75% of its games, how many games did the team play? _____

B. Henry has 4 pitchers on his team that make up 16% of the team. How many players are on Henry's team? _____

Name/Date _____

Find a Number When a Percent of It Is Known 4

The seventh-grade class was having a bake sale.

They were selling crispy treats, brownies, and cookies. In the first two hours of the sale, they sold $45. This was 12% of the baked goods for sale. How much money could they potentially make at the sale? _____

Name/Date _____

Find a Number When a Percent Of It Is Known 5

A. At the Chess State Championship, Lester scored 35 points, which was 28% of the team's total points. How many points did the team score in all? _____

B. Liz has run 1,600 miles of her annual mileage goal. If this is 80% of her annual goal, how many miles does she plan to run this year? _____

C. The population of the city of Washington (located in Wayne County) is 5,091, or 15%, of the total population of Wayne County. What is the population of Wayne County? _____

Math Word Problems Warm-ups: Find a Percent of Increase or Decrease

Name/Date _____

Find a Percent of Increase or Decrease 1

A. Ralph's Potato Chips increased the size of their bags from 12 ounces to 16 ounces. What is the percent of increase in the size of the bag? Round your answer to the nearest percent. _____

B. Tasty Juice surveyed their customers and found that customers preferred to have smaller containers of juice. Tasty Juice reduced the size from 48 ounces to 16 ounces. What is the percent of decrease? Round your answer to the nearest percent. _____

Name/Date _____

Find a Percent of Increase or Decrease 2

The ticket price to the amusement park increased from $35 to $40. What is the percent of increase? Round your answer to the nearest percent.

_____

Name/Date _____

Find a Percent of Increase or Decrease 3

A. At Carla's old job, she earned $7.25 per hour. Now she earns $8.00. What is the percent of increase in her hourly wage? Round your answer to the nearest percent. _____

B. Also, Carla traveled 35 miles to work for her old job. Now she only has to drive 7 miles to work. What is the percent of decrease in miles?

_____

Name/Date _____

Find a Percent of Increase or Decrease 4

Last year, the Tigers basketball team won 24 out of 30 games. This year, they won 28 out of 30 games. What is the percent of increase in games won? Round your answer to the nearest percent. _____

Name/Date _____

Find a Percent of Increase or Decrease 5

An automobile manufacturer reported that truck sales have decreased from 12,218 in July to 10,398 in August. What is the percent of decrease in truck sales? Round your answer to the nearest percent. _____

Math Word Problems Warm-ups: Using Percents

Name/Date _____

Using Percents 1

A. Stacy has baked 20% of the cookies for the bake sale. If she needs to bake 15 dozen cookies, how many more dozen cookies does she need to bake? _____

B. While baking, she burned $1\frac{1}{2}$ dozen cookies. What is the percent of decrease in the number of cookies from the total? _____

Name/Date _____

Using Percents 2

A. At the animal shelter, 20 out of 50 animals are dogs. What percent of the animals are dogs? _____

B. The shelter found homes for 22 out of 50 cats and dogs. This was an increase from the prior month where the shelter found homes for only 12 out of 50 cats and dogs. What was the percent of increase? Round your answer to the nearest percent. _____

Name/Date _____

Using Percents 3

A. The Montclair Drum and Bugle Corps has 54 drummers, who make up 45% of the members. How many members are in the Montclair Drum and Bugle Corps?

_____

B. The team needs new uniforms. They have raised $2,700 out of $45,000. What percent of the $45,000 did the team raise? _____

C. The members had a concert to raise money for the uniforms. They raised 22% of the total amount needed. How much money did they raise from the concert? _____

Name/Date _____

Using Percents 4

The Spino family is driving to Yellowstone National Park, a distance of 832 miles. On the first day, they drive 30% of the total distance. How many miles did they drive on the first day?

_____

Name/Date _____

Using Percents 5

A. Zac's hockey team ended their season with 7 wins and 9 losses. What percent of the games did the team win? _____
What percent did they lose? _____

B. Zac had assists in 13 of the 16 games. In what percentage of the games did Zac have assists? Round your answer to the nearest whole number. _____

Math Word Problems Warm-ups: Discounts and Sale Prices

Name/Date _____

Discounts and Sale Prices 1

Michel had a coupon for $\frac{1}{3}$ off the price of a large pizza. If a large pizza is $16.95, how much money will Michel save using the coupon?

_____

Name/Date _____

Discounts and Sale Prices 2

Tony found some sunglasses for $136 at a local store. Tony found the same pair on the Internet for half the price of the local store as well as free shipping and a 20% discount. Next week, the local store is having a big blowout sale—everything 65% off. Which is the better sales price? _____

Name/Date _____

Discounts and Sale Prices 3

Renee bought a picture on sale for $75.60. She received 20% off the discounted price and 25% off the original price. What was the original price of the picture? _____

Name/Date _____

Discounts and Sale Prices 4

The original cost for a baseball mitt and baseball is $36. The mitt is three times as expensive as the baseball. Lee has a coupon for $\frac{1}{4}$ off the baseball and 40% off the mitt. What is the total sales price?

_____

Name/Date _____

_____

Discounts and Sale Prices 5

A. The Running Store was having a sale of 30% off all shoes. Tyler found a pair of track shoes. The original price is $98. What is the sale price? _____

B. Vlad needs two oriental rugs cleaned. Arax Oriental Rug Cleaning estimated $220–$250 for one rug and $55–$65 for the other rug. Vlad can receive a 20% discount if he brings both rugs to Arax. How much money could Vlad potentially save if he brings the rugs to Arax? _____

C. At the camping sale, Wendy bought a tent for $148 that originally cost $185, not including tax. The store had the same discount on sleeping bags. What is the sale price of a sleeping bag that originally costs $235?

_____

Math Word Problems Warm-ups: Sales Tax

Name/Date _____

Sales Tax 1

A. Phillip works at a bookstore. A customer buys a book for $25. Phillip needs to add 8% sales tax to the price of the book. What is the amount of sales tax? _____ What should Phillip charge the customer for the book, including tax? _____

B. Marvin went to dinner with his family. The bill came to $55. The sales tax was 6%. What was the total cost for dinner? _____

Name/Date _____

Sales Tax 2

A. Tammy buys a shirt for $12 and a skirt for $23. Sales tax is 5%. How much sales tax will Tammy have to pay? _____ What will be the total cost of her purchases? _____

B. Reggie wants to buy a snowboard for $230. He has $240 in his savings account. His mother tells him he has to pay 7% sales tax. Does Reggie have enough money to purchase the snowboard? _____ By how much? _____

Name/Date _____

Sales Tax 3

A. Craig needs a new pair of running shoes. The local store has the brand he wants for $125. If he buys them on the Internet, there is no sales tax and free shipping. Sales tax is 5.25%. How much money can Craig save in sales tax by buying them on the Internet? Round your answer to the nearest cent. _____

B. Megan bought a lamp for a total of $37.10, including tax. If she paid $2.10 in sales tax, what was the price of the lamp? _____ What was the sales tax rate? _____

Name/Date _____

Sales Tax 4

A. Kari bought a purse for $12 that was originally $38, not including tax. If the sales tax is 4.5%, how much money did Kari save in sales tax by buying at the sale price? _____

B. Curt ordered a rug for $29.90 plus 8.25% sales tax. The shipping fee was $6.50. Sales tax is not applied to shipping fees. What was the total cost of the rug, including tax and shipping? _____

Name/Date _____

Sales Tax 5

The sales clerk at the appliance store added 5% sales tax to the cost of the washing machine. He then charged an additional $75 for delivery and $10 to dispose of the old washing machine. The clerk told Molly the total was $499.75. What was the price of the washing machine? _____

Math Word Problems Warm-ups: Discounts, Sale Price, & Sales Tax

Name/Date _____

Discounts, Sale Price, & Sales Tax 1

Scott saw a suit on clearance for $385. If Scott purchases the suit with his store credit card, he gets an additional 10% off the clearance price.

A. What is the sale price? _____

B. Sales tax is 5.75%. What is the total price of the suit, including tax? _____

Name/Date _____

Discounts, Sale Price, & Sales Tax 2

Leslie saw a dress on sale for $43 and a handbag on sale for $35. She also has a coupon for an extra 10% off clothing and 20% off handbags.

A. What is the sale price of the dress? _____ Handbag? _____

B. Sales tax is 8.75%. What is the total cost, including tax? _____

Name/Date _____

Discounts, Sale Price, & Sales Tax 3

A. Tonerland advertised 59% off toner cartridges. If the regular price were $58.37, how much would you save if you bought one cartridge?

_____

B. If sales tax is 7%, what is the total cost of one cartridge? _____

Name/Date _____

Discounts, Sale Price, & Sales Tax 4

Big Sports has a tent, which was originally $129.99, on sale for $79. Lisa has a coupon for $\frac{1}{2}$ off the sale price and has only fifty dollars to spend.

A. If sales tax is 8%, does she have enough money to buy the tent? _____

B. By how much? _____

Name/Date _____

Discounts, Sale Price, & Sales Tax 5

Sara found a pair of jeans for $48 with a sticker on the tag: "Take an additional 25% off." When Sara went to pay for the jeans, the clerk told her that the jeans were going on clearance tomorrow for 65% off the reduced price. Sara waited and bought the jeans the following day.

A. If sales tax was 6%, what was the total cost of the jeans? _____

B. How much money did she save by waiting a day, including tax? _____

Math Word Problems Warm-ups: Simple Interest on Savings

Name/Date _____

Simple Interest on Savings 1

A. Juanita bought a 6-month certificate of deposit (CD) for $1,000. The yearly interest rate on the CD is 4.75%. How much will the CD be worth in six months? _____

B. Irene earned $180 mowing lawns. She puts half of her earnings in a savings account that earns 5.2% interest yearly. How much interest will she earn at the end of three months? _____

Name/Date _____

Simple Interest on Savings 2

Raquel put her babysitting earnings of $236 in a savings account at an interest rate of 5%.

A. Assuming the interest rate does not change, and she does not deposit more money, how much interest will she earn on this money at the end of five years? _____

B. What will be her savings account balance at the end of five years? _____

Name/Date _____

Simple Interest on Savings 3

Harry earned $525 by mowing lawns over the last two months. He put the money in a savings account, which earns 4% per year.

A. Assuming interest rates do not change, how much interest will he earn on this money at the end of the year? _____

B. What will be his savings account balance at the end of the year? _____

Name/Date _____

Simple Interest on Savings 4

Jorge earns $203 per month delivering newspapers. He put 6 months' earnings into a money market fund 18 months ago. The interest rate on the account was 5.5% per year. Then he used the interest he earned to buy a stereo.

How much could he spend on the stereo? Round your answer to the nearest cent.

_____

Name/Date _____

Simple Interest on Savings 5

Ms. Bateman plans to use the interest she earns in her savings account to pay for a trip to San Francisco, which costs $540. She has $4,000 in her savings account at 6% per year.

Assuming the interest rate does not change, how long will it take her to save for the trip?

_____

Math Word Problems Warm-ups: Simple Interest on Loans

Name/Date _____

Simple Interest on Loans 1

Mr. Nichols borrowed $578 for car repairs. The interest rate is 23% per year. It takes Mr. Nicholas 3 years to pay off this loan.

A. How much interest did he pay? _____

B. What was the total amount he paid?

_____

Name/Date _____

Simple Interest on Loans 2

Mr. Palma borrowed $9,500 to purchase a car. The loan is for 36 months, and the interest rate is 6.38% per year.

A. How much interest will he pay?

_____

B. What will be the total amount he pays for the car at the end of three years?

_____

Name/Date _____

Simple Interest on Loans 3

Shaniqua bought a bed for $695 and a dresser for $395, including tax. She put $165 down and financed the remaining amount at 5.4% interest for $3\frac{1}{2}$ years.

A. How much interest did she save by putting $165 down? Round to the nearest cent.

_____

Darla bought a new couch for $895, including tax. Designer Furniture offers two financing options: 5.3% interest for 18 months or 4.8% interest for 2 years.

B. Which is the better deal? _____

C. How much interest would Darla save if she took the better deal? _____

Name/Date _____

Simple Interest on Loans 4

Ursula bought a mattress and box springs for $899, including tax. She paid $150 and financed the remaining amount at an interest rate of 5.3% for 6 months. What was the total amount she paid for the mattress and box springs?

_____

Name/Date _____

Simple Interest on Loans 5

A. It took Hiroko 4 years to pay off her student loan. The interest rate on the loan was 8%. She paid $800 in interest over the life of the loan. What was the original amount of the loan? _____

B. Jamal's parents borrowed $3,000 to replace windows in their home. Over the life of the loan, they paid $585 in interest at a yearly rate of 6.5%. How long did it take them to pay off the loan? _____

     35

Math Word Problems Warm-ups: Profit

Name/Date _____

Profit 1

Freddie put on a volleyball tournament to raise money for the 21st Street Volleyball Club. The registration fee was $15, and each participant would receive a T-shirt. It cost Freddie $4 for each shirt. Sixty-three people played in the tournament. How much money did Freddie raise after expenses?

_____

Name/Date _____

Profit 2

Maria and Beth decide to sell bracelets at the school carnival for $0.50 each. It costs $0.10 to make each bracelet.

A. If they sell 35 bracelets, how much money will they make after costs? _____

B. What is the least number of bracelets they need to sell in order to make a $25 profit?

_____

Name/Date _____

Profit 3

A hat company can make hats for $2 each. The company's other costs are about $400 per day. They sell the hats for $5.50 each. If it took the company three days to sell 2,000 hats, what was their profit?

_____

Name/Date _____

Profit 4

An electronics company makes circuit boards for $1 each and sells them for $6 each. Their business expenses are $900 per day. Their goal is to make a profit of 15% more than their daily business expenses.

A. What is the least number of circuit boards they must sell to meet their goal? _____

B. If they sell 2,600 circuit boards in one week (5 working days), what was their profit? _____

Name/Date _____

Profit 5

Jeanine is looking for a part-time job. She interviews at the pet shop a few blocks from her home. This job pays $6.90 per hour, and she would work 4 hours a day, 3 days a week. Then she interviews for a job as a sales clerk, which pays $7.50 per hour, and she would work 3 hours a day, 4 days a week. Also for the sales job, Jeanine would need to take the bus to and from work, at a cost of $1.20 each way.

A. Which job would be more profitable? _____

B. How much more would Jeanine make per week? _____

Math Word Problems Warm-ups:
Add and Subtract Integers

Name/Date _____

Add and Subtract Integers 1

A. Jude weighs 180 pounds. He wants to lose 20 pounds, so he began exercising and eating healthily. He weighs himself once a week. The first week he lost 3 pounds, but the second week he gained 1 pound. How many weeks will it take him to reach his goal if he continues to gain and lose weight in this same pattern? _____

B. The top of a house is 32 feet above ground level. The basement of the house goes to a depth of 9 feet below ground level (-9). What is the difference between the height of the house and the depth of the basement? _____

Name/Date _____

Add and Subtract Integers 2

The temperature was -2°F at 6:00 a.m. By noon, the temperature had risen 15 degrees. Between noon and 6:00 p.m., the temperature dropped 8 degrees. What was the temperature at 6:00 p.m.?

_____

Name/Date _____

Add and Subtract Integers 3

At the beginning of last month, the price of gasoline was $2.37 per gallon. It increased $0.07, decreased $0.05, increased $0.10, decreased $0.03, decreased $0.08, and increased $0.13. What is the total increase or decrease in price? Write your answer as an integer. _____

Name/Date _____

Add and Subtract Integers 4

The Tigers have the football on the opposing team's 30-yard line. The Tigers gained 5 yards on their first play, but lost 7 yards on their second play. Then on their third play they gained 3 yards. What is the total yardage gained or lost? Write your answer as an integer. _____

Name/Date _____

Add and Subtract Integers 5

Hannah bought one share of stock in CompuNational for $4 a share. The change in the price of a share was +$0.50 the following day. The next day, the change was -$5. What is her one share of stock worth now? _____

Math Word Problems Warm-ups: Multiply and Divide Integers

Name/Date _____

Multiply and Divide Integers 1

A. Carl is on a hot-air balloon ride. His balloon has been rising at an average rate of 3 feet per second. If the current rate continues, how many feet will he have risen in 2 minutes? Write your answer as an integer.

_____

B. Carl's balloon ride is over. The balloon begins its descent at a rate of 5 feet per second. If the current rate continues, how many feet will it have descended in 5 minutes? Write your answer as an integer.

_____

Name/Date _____

Multiply and Divide Integers 2

The temperature in Roxbury decreased 15°F in five hours. What was the average decrease in temperature per hour? Write your answer as an integer. _____

Name/Date _____

Multiply and Divide Integers 3

The Lions quarterback was sacked on the last 3 plays. The team lost 5 yards each time the quarterback was sacked. By how many yards did the Lions' total yardage change because of quarterback sacks? Write your answer as an integer.

_____

Name/Date _____

Multiply and Divide Integers 4

A toy store's stock was down -102 points over the last three days. What was the average decrease for the three days? Write your answer as an integer. _____

Name/Date _____

Multiply and Divide Integers 5

Mr. Smith owns a toy business. His sales have been decreasing at an average rate of 1,253 units per year for the last seven years. What is the total decrease over this time period? Write your answer as an integer. _____

Math Word Problems Warm-ups: Averages

Averages 1

A. Kathy bought five shirts. The prices of the shirts were: $7, $12, $15, $18, and $21. What is the mean price of the shirts? _____

B. Eight adults together spent $294.72 on dinner. What was the mean amount spent by each person? _____

Averages 2

A. Callie bought four CDs. The CDs cost $17.89, $12.36, $10.96, and $13.07. What is the mean price of the CDs? _____

B. Over the past six months, the city of Branton accumulated a total of 29.76 inches of rain. What is the average monthly rainfall?

_____

Averages 3

A. Ms. Mallory recorded the heights of the girls' volleyball team. Four girls were 72", two girls were 74", three girls were 69", and two girls were 71". What is the mean of the girls' heights? Round your answer to the nearest hundredth. _____

B. Tia took a survey of the number of pets in her classmates' households. Six students have one pet, six students have two pets, four students have three pets, and four students have no pets. What is the mean number of pets in households for this class? _____

Averages 4

The basketball team plays in a tournament. The team's points for the first five games are 76, 52, 63, 84, and 73. The team will play a sixth game. The team must have a mean of 70 for the six games to advance to the next round. How many points will the team have to score in the sixth game to advance to the next round?

_____

Averages 5

Wilson Middle School's play was for seven nights. The mean number of tickets sold was 190 tickets. Ticket sales for the first five nights were 188, 190, 192, 185, and 183. What was the mean number of tickets sold for the last two nights? _____

Math Word Problems Warm-ups: Permutations and Combinations

Name/Date _____

Permutations and Combinations 1

A. Melanie needed to put a tablecloth on two tables. She had 1 red tablecloth, 1 blue tablecloth, 1 checked tablecloth, and 1 polka-dotted tablecloth to choose from. How many different selections are possible? _____

B. Ms. Spencer was making the schedule for Friday's night performances. The acts are: magician, comedian, singer, and dancer. How many different ways can she schedule the performances so that the magician and comedian will not perform after or before each other? _____

Name/Date _____

Permutations and Combinations 2

A. Matt has 4 trophies—hockey, baseball, soccer, and water polo—sitting on a shelf in his bedroom. How many different ways can he arrange the 4 trophies in a row? _____

B. Granny's Deli offers turkey, tuna, ham, or pastrami sandwiches on rye, wheat, white, or sourdough bread. How many possible sandwich combinations does Granny's Deli offer? _____

Name/Date _____

Permutations and Combinations 3

Michael is on vacation. He wants to see the castle, take a boat ride, and visit the museum, Roman baths, a cathedral, and Botanical Gardens. But he does not have time to do all six activities. He can only do 3 activities. How many different selections of 3 sightseeing options are possible? _____

Name/Date _____

Permutations and Combinations 4

At the annual golf tournament, Kevin, Devin, Tonya, Natalie, and Seth were the five finalists. Identical first, second, and third prizes were awarded among the 5 finalists. How many different ways are possible for the 3 prizes to be awarded? _____

Name/Date _____

Permutations and Combinations 5

There are 10 cars in the running for the best car of the year award. But first, three cars are to be selected as finalists. How many ways can this initial selection occur? _____

Math Word Problems Warm-ups: Probability

Name/Date _____

Probability 1

A. Shane has a bag containing 3 blue, 2 yellow, 4 green, and 3 red marbles. If he randomly chooses one marble from the bag, what is the probability the marble will be green? _____

B. Aaron puts 4 red socks and 3 blue socks into a bag. If Aaron picks a sock from the bag without looking and then returns the sock to the bag twenty-one times, what is the number of times that he can expect to pick a red sock? _____

Name/Date _____

Probability 2

A. The letters M I S S I S S I P P I are each written on a card and placed in a bag. If Wanda picks a card from the bag without looking, what is the probability that the card she chooses shows an "S"? _____

B. Lillian loves to play her trivia game. She wins 3 out of every 4 games she plays. How many games would she be expected to win if she played 428 games? _____

Name/Date _____

Probability 3

A. A bag of candy has 4 green, 3 red, 8 yellow, 6 brown, 5 orange, and 4 blue candies. If Walter randomly chooses one candy from the bag, what's the probability of Walter getting an orange candy? _____

B. Logan is one of the best hitters on his baseball team. He usually gets a hit 2 out of every 3 times at bat. If Logan were to bat 180 times, how many hits would be expected? _____

Name/Date _____

Probability 4

A. Jessie usually gets 5 aces out of every 8 serves. During the volleyball season, she serves 136 times. How many ace serves would she be expected to get? _____

B. The farmer puts 7 apples, 10 pears, and 5 oranges in a basket. If his wife were to randomly choose one piece of fruit from the basket, what is the probability she would get a pear? _____

Name/Date _____

Probability 5

A. There are 5 chocolate bars and 3 coconut bars in a bag. If Mary picks a candy bar from the bag without looking and then returns the candy bar to the bag 120 times, what is the number of times that she can expect to pick a chocolate bar? _____

B. In a survey, 30 customers were asked what kind of muffin they would buy. The results showed 9 blueberry, 8 pumpkin, 6 lemon, and 7 chocolate chip. Based on this survey, how many of 180 customers would probably buy pumpkin? _____

Math Word Problems Warm-ups: Answer Keys

Add & Subtract Whole Numbers 1 (p. 3)
6,904 dolls

Add & Subtract Whole Numbers 2 (p. 3)
22 pages

Add & Subtract Whole Numbers 3 (p. 3)
27,777 vehicles

Add & Subtract Whole Numbers 4 (p. 3)
1,075 miles

Add & Subtract Whole Numbers 5 (p. 3)
A. 348 flowers
B. 108 boys and 81 girls

Multiply and Divide Whole Numbers 1 (p. 4)
A. 240 comic books
B. 52 boxes (51.8 rounded up)

Multiply and Divide Whole Numbers 2 (p. 4)
180 days

Multiply and Divide Whole Numbers 3 (p. 4)
A. Zac   B. 6 slices

Multiply and Divide Whole Numbers 4 (p. 4)
10,920 cases

Multiply and Divide Whole Numbers 5 (p. 4)
Lou and Tyra (300 apples)

All Operations Whole Numbers 1 (p. 5)
A. boys: 4, girls: 2
B. 13 6-cookie packages,
   15 2-cookie packages

All Operations Whole Numbers 2 (p. 5)
5

All Operations Whole Numbers 3 (p. 5)
A. Henry   B. 171 pages

All Operations Whole Numbers 4 (p. 5)
A. 22 days   B. 8 days

All Operations Whole Numbers 5 (p. 5)
Sixth grade, 101 sixth graders

Add & Subtract Decimals 1 (p. 6)
Kelly, 5.16

Add & Subtract Decimals 2 (p. 6)
83.8

Add & Subtract Decimals 3 (p. 6)
79.45 points

Add & Subtract Decimals 4 (p. 6)
4.48 in. Renton; 2.28 in. Stampede Pass; 1.4 in. Bellingham; 5.39 in. Hoquiam

Add & Subtract Decimals 5 (p. 6)
A. 31.92 miles;
B. $1.29 box of pasta,
   $2.47 jar of tomato sauce

Multiply & Divide Decimals 1 (p. 7)
31,304 points

Multiply & Divide Decimals 2 (p. 7)
96 flowers

Multiply & Divide Decimals 3 (p. 7)
6.99 minutes

Multiply & Divide Decimals 4 (p. 7)
≈2.54 kilowatts per day

Multiply & Divide Decimals 5 (p. 7)
A. 52 gallons
B. 3.25 tanks of gas

All Operations Decimals 1 (p. 8)
A. 17,600 units   B. 3.6 liters

All Operations Decimals 2 (p. 8)
2,252.88 miles

All Operations Decimals 3 (p. 8)
9.45 miles

All Operations Decimals 4 (p. 8)
9 weeks

All Operations Decimals 5 (p. 8)
Team North won by 1.15 seconds.

Add & Subtract Fractions 1 (p. 9)
A. $\frac{6}{35}$ B. $\frac{9}{6}$ or $1\frac{1}{2}$

Add & Subtract Fractions 2 (p. 9)
A. $7\frac{4}{7}$ B. $3\frac{33}{56}$

Add & Subtract Fractions 3 (p. 9)
$6\frac{3}{8}$ miles

Add & Subtract Fractions 4 (p. 9)
$\frac{2}{3}$ cup

Add & Subtract Fractions 5 (p. 9)
A. $\frac{7}{8}$ B. $5\frac{1}{24}$ miles; $8\frac{1}{8}$ miles

Multiply & Divide Fractions 1 (p. 10)
A. $\frac{1}{10}$ acre   B. 11

Multiply & Divide Fractions 2 (p. 10)
A. 9 days
B. 35 dogs, 25 cats, 15 other animals

Multiply & Divide Fractions 3 (p. 10)
A. $\frac{1}{6}$ brother, $\frac{1}{10}$ mom
B. $13\frac{3}{4}$ hours

Multiply & Divide Fractions 4 (p. 10)
$\frac{5}{8}''$

Multiply & Divide Fractions 5 (p. 10)
6 containers

All Operations With Fractions 1 (p. 11)
A. 4; B. less, $2\frac{1}{8}$ yards

All Operations With Fractions 2 (p. 11)
father 36 years old, Charles 12 years old

All Operations With Fractions 3 (p. 11)
609 seats

All Operations With Fractions 4 (p. 11)
A. 24 muffins
B. Steve 3, Dori 7, Sheila 2

All Operations With Fractions 5 (p. 11)
$13\frac{3}{8}''$

Money 1 (p. 12)
A. $10.09   B. $0.69

Money 2 (p. 12)
A. 1 quarter, 3 dimes, 1 nickel, 1 penny
B. 4 fives, 8 ones

Money 3 (p. 12)
A. $53.50   B. 187 minutes

Money 4 (p. 12)
A. $3.95   B. $3.75

Money 5 (p. 12)
A. 56 students, 7 adults
B. Mindy $30, Max $75

Customary Units of Measurement 1 (p. 13)
A. 16 feet
B. Alonzo 4 ounces, Latrell 12 ounces

Customary Units of Measurement 2 (p. 13)
A. 8 inches   B. 56 sandwiches

Customary Units of Measurement 3 (p. 13)
A. $4.60   B. 1 quart, 3 cups

Customary Units of Measurement 4 (p. 13)
264 sections

Customary Units of Measurement 5 (p. 13)
A. 14 ounces
B. 32 quarts, 32 pints

Metric Units of Measurement 1 (p. 14)
A. 14 liters   B. ≈28.57 beads
C. 20 containers
D. 27 kilometers

Metric Units of Measurement 2 (p. 14)
6 packages

Metric Units of Measurement 3 (p. 14)
6 two-liter servings

Metric Units of Measurement 4 (p. 14)
1 liter, 925 milliliters

Metric Units of Measurement 5 (p. 14)
3.41 m

Time 1 (p. 15)
2 hours 45 minutes

Time 2 (p. 15)
A. 8:30 a.m.
B. 3 hours 15 minutes

Time 3 (p. 15)
A. 9 hours 30 minutes
B. 9:45 a.m., 1:15 p.m.

Time 4 (p. 15)
6:13 p.m.

Time 5 (p. 15)
A. 4 hours 47 minutes
B. 3:57 p.m.

Using Measurement 1 (p. 16)
A. 20 feet 8 inches   B. 18 days

Using Measurement 2 (p. 16)
A. $3\frac{1}{2}$ quarts   B. 132 kilometers

Using Measurement 3 (p. 16)
A. 6:18 p.m.
B. Rochelle, 500 milliliters or 0.5 or $\frac{1}{2}$ liters more

Using Measurement 4 (p. 16)
A. 29 cups   B. 8 cups

Using Measurement 5 (p. 16)
A. 8:50 p.m.
B. 9 pounds, 10 ounces

Angles 1 (p. 17)
A. 109°   B. 40°

Angles 2 (p. 17)
A. 119°   B. 22°

Angles 3 (p. 17)
A. 65°   B. 105°

Angles 4 (p. 17)
37°

Angles 5 (p. 17)
80°

Perimeter and Area of Quadrilaterals 1 (p. 18)
A. 28.8 meters   B. 133 feet

Perimeter and Area of Quadrilaterals 2 (p. 18)
A. 324 square inches
B. 36 inches

Perimeter and Area of Quadrilaterals 3 (p. 18)
2 cans (It will take 1.08 cans.)

Perimeter and Area of Quadrilaterals 4 (p. 18)
A. 9 pieces (It will take 8.38 pieces)
B. 324 square feet

Perimeter and Area of Quadrilaterals 5 (p. 18)
208 yards

Circumference and Area of Circles 1 (p. 19)
A. about 36 inches
B. about 42.39 inches

Circumference and Area of Circles 2 (p. 19)
smallest silo about 50.24 feet, medium silo about 62.8 feet, large silo about 75.36 feet

Circumference and Area of Circles 3 (p. 19)
A. about 25.12 feet
B. about 50.24 feet

Circumference and Area of Circles 4 (p. 19)
A. about 21.98 square feet
B. about 32 inches

Circumference and Area of Circles 5 (p. 19)
A. about 530.66 square feet, about 81.64 feet
B. about 452.16 square inches

Volume 1 (p. 20)
2,520 cubic centimeters

Volume 2 (p. 20)
91.845 cubic centimeters

Volume 3 (p. 20)
A. 144   B. 8 feet

Volume 4 (p. 20)
29.83 cubic inches

Volume 5 (p. 20)
1,200 cubic inches

Surface Area 1 (p. 21)
62 square feet

Surface Area 2 (p. 21)
78 square yards

Surface Area 3 (p. 21)
2,512 square centimeters

Surface Area 4 (p. 21)
A. 6 centimeters
B. 25 centimeters

Surface Area 5 (p. 21)
A. 942 square inches
B. 8 inches

Ratios 1 (p. 22)
A. 33:18   B. 7:15

Ratios 2 (p. 22)
A. 9:20   B. 5:12, 3:17

Ratios 3 (p. 22)
A. 9:12
B. 206 hot lunches, 154 sack lunches
C. 35 dogs
D. 20 cats

Ratios 4 (p. 22)
A. 12:18:5   B. 5:35

Ratios 5 (p. 22)
A. Brad 48 student votes, Alice 80 student votes

Proportions 1 (p. 23)
A. 60 chaperons   B. 135 boys

Proportions 2 (p. 23)
A. 6″ wide

Proportions 3 (p. 23)
A. 140 miles   B. 10 servings

Proportions 4 (p. 23)
A. 72 ounces of orange juice, 24 ounces of grapefruit juice

Proportions 5 (p. 23)
A. 166,800   B. 12 days

Unit Prices 1 (p. 24)
A. $0.33   B. $1.25   C. $2.75

Unit Prices 2 (p. 24)
A. $14.26   B. 2.38 pounds

Unit Prices 3 (p. 24)
A. $14.55
B. 6-pack at $4.33 per lightbulb

Unit Prices 4 (p. 24)
A. three 64-ounce cans
B. $3 roses, $2 tulips

Unit Prices 5 (p. 24)
A. Two 2.5 gallons
B. $2.50 per blouse, $3.25 per dress

Fractions, Decimals, and Percents 1 (p. 25)
A. pizza
B. most: country, least: classical

Fractions, Decimals, and Percents 2 (p. 25)
Aaron

Fractions, Decimals, and Percents 3 (p. 25)
A. $\frac{70}{100}$ or 7/10, 0.7
B. playing games and food and drinks

Fractions, Decimals, and Percents 4 (p. 25)
A. 130   B. 234   C. 156

Fractions, Decimals, and Percents 5 (p. 25)
A. Tara and Shane   B. Tony
C. 20 cars

Find Percents of Numbers 1 (p. 26)
A. $1,125   B. 4 weeks
C. 9.6 feet

Find Percents of Numbers 2 (p. 26)
A. 436 seats
B. 49 swans, 98 ducks, 53 geese

Find Percents of Numbers 3 (p. 26)
A. 15 students
B. 108 students
C. 105 students

Find Percents of Numbers 4 (p. 26)
$294.25

Find Percents of Numbers 5 (p. 26)
A. 5.85″ x 9.75″   B. 1,769

Find a Percent 1 (p. 27)
A. 77%   B. 40%

Find a Percent 2 (p. 27)
A. 79%   B. 45%

Find a Percent 3 (p. 27)
A. 75%   B. 88%

Find a Percent 4 (p. 27)
A. 30%   B. 50%

Find a Percent 5 (p. 27)
A. 83%   B. 17%

Find a Number When a Percent of It Is Known 1 (p. 28)
A. $3,500   B. $2,275

Find a Number When a Percent of It Is Known 2 (p. 28)
A. 145   B. 128

Find a Number When a Percent of It Is Known 3 (p. 28)
A. 48 games   B. 25 players

Find a Number When a Percent of It Is Known 4 (p. 28)
$375

Find a Number When a Percent of It Is Known 5 (p. 28)
A. 125 points   B. 2,000 miles
C. 33,940

Find a Percent of Increase or Decrease 1 (p. 29)
A. 33%   B. 67%

Find a Percent of Increase or Decrease 2 (p. 29)
14%

Find a Percent of Increase or Decrease 3 (p. 29)
A. 10%   B. 80%

Find a Percent of Increase or Decrease 4 (p. 29)
13%

Find a Percent of Increase or Decrease 5 (p. 29)
15%

Using Percents 1 (p. 30)
A. 12 dozen   B. 10%

Using Percents 2 (p. 30)
A. 40%   B. 20%

Using Percents 3 (p. 30)
A. 120 members
B. 6%   C. $9,900

Using Percents 4 (p. 30)
249.6 miles

Using Percents 5 (p. 30)
A. 44% wins, 56% losses
B. 81.25%

Discounts and Sale Prices 1 (p. 31)
$5.65

Discounts and Sale Prices 2 (p. 31)
Local store for $47.60

Discounts and Sale Prices 3 (p. 31)
$126

Discounts and Sale Prices 4 (p. 31)
$22.95

Discounts and Sale Prices 5 (p. 31)
A. $68.60   B. $55-$63
C. $188

Sales Tax 1 (p. 32)
A. $2, $27   B. $58.30

Sales Tax 2 (p. 32)
A. $1.75, $36.75
B. No, he needs $6.10 more

Sales Tax 3 (p. 32)
A. $6.56   B. $35, 5.66%

Sales Tax 4 (p. 32)
A. $1.17   B. $38.87

Sales Tax 5 (p. 32)
$395

Discounts, Sale Price, & Sales Tax 1 (p. 33)
A. $346.50   B. $366.42

Discounts, Sale Price, & Sales Tax 2 (p. 33)
A. dress: $38.70, handbag: $28
B. $72.54

Discounts, Sale Price, & Sales Tax 3 (p. 33)
A. $34.44   B. $25.61

Discounts, Sale Price, & Sales Tax 4 (p. 33)
A. Yes
B. She has $7.34 more.

Discounts, Sale Price, & Sales Tax 5 (p. 33)
A. $13.36   B. $24.80

Simple Interest on Savings 1 (p. 34)
A. $1,023.75 B. $1.17

Simple Interest on Savings 2 (p. 34)
A. $59   B. $295

Simple Interest on Savings 3 (p. 34)
A. $21   B. $546

Simple Interest on Savings 4 (p. 34)
$100.49

Simple Interest on Savings 5 (p. 34)
2 years, 3 months

Simple Interest on Loans 1 (p. 35)
A. $398.82   B. $976.82

Simple Interest on Loans 2 (p. 35)
A. $1,818.30   B. $11,318.30

Simple Interest on Loans 3 (p. 35)
A. $31.19
B. 5.3% interest for 18 months
C. $14.77

Simple Interest on Loans 4 (p. 35)
$918.85

Simple Interest on Loans 5 (p. 35)
A. $2,500   B. 3 years

Profit 1 (p. 36)
$693

Profit 2 (p. 36)
A. $14   B. 63 bracelets

Profit 3 (p. 36)
$5,800

Profit 4 (p. 36)
A. 207 circuit boards
B. $8,500

Profit 5 (p. 36)
A. Pet Shop   B. $2.40

Add & Subtract Integers 1 (p. 36)
A. ≈20 weeks B. 41 feet

Add & Subtract Integers 2 (p. 37)
+5°F

Add & Subtract Integers 3 (p. 37)
+$0.14

Add & Subtract Integers 4 (p. 37)
+1 yard

Add & Subtract Integers 5 (p. 37)
-$0.50

Multiply & Divide Integers 1 (p. 38)
A. +360 feet   B. -1500 feet

Multiply & Divide Integers 2 (p. 38)
-3°F per hour

Multiply & Divide Integers 3 (p. 38)
-15 yards

Multiply & Divide Integers 4 (p. 38)
-34 points

Multiply & Divide Integers 5 (p. 38)
-8,771 units

Averages 1 (p. 39)
A. $14.60   B. $36.84

Averages 2 (p. 39)
A. $13.57
B. 4.96 inches of rain

Averages 3 (p. 39)
A. 71.36″   B. 1.5

Averages 4 (p. 39)
72 points

Averages 5 (p. 39)
196

Permutations & Combinations 1 (p. 40)
A. 12   B. 12

Permutations & Combinations 2 (p. 40)
A. 24   B. 16

Permutations & Combinations 3 (p. 40)
20

Permutations & Combinations 4 (p. 40)
60

Permutations & Combinations 5 (p. 40)
120

Probability 1 (p. 41)
A. $\frac{4}{12}$ or $\frac{1}{3}$ B. 12 times

Probability 2 (p. 41)
A. $\frac{4}{11}$ B. 321 games

Probability 3 (p. 41)
A. $\frac{5}{30}$ or $\frac{1}{6}$ B. 120 hits

Probability 4 (p. 41)
A. 85   B. $\frac{10}{22}$ or $\frac{5}{11}$

Probability 5 (p. 41)
A. 75   B. 48